The Uncertainty from Anxiety

Jeffery Parasram

The Uncertainty from Anxiety

All poems are catalog with the Library of Congress. 101 Independence Avenue, South East, Washington D.C. 20559

Front cover art by Torre Howard

All rights reserved. No part of this publication may be reproduced, stored in a retrieval system, or transmitted in any form or by any means. For example, electronic, photocopy, recording-without prior written permission from the author. The only exception is brief quotations in printed reviews.

Copyright © 2021 Jeffery Parasram

All rights reserved.

ISBN: 978-1-7379666-0-9

The Uncertainty from Anxiety

DEDICATION

The Uncertainty from Anxiety is dedicated to my mother Evelyn Parasram for showing me to believe in myself and for reaching for the stars.

And in memory of my father Cecil Parasram who encourage me to greet *life* with humor and not to take it for granted.

Jeffery Parasram

About The Author

    For many years I suffered from anxiety. I called it the *silent taker*. It took away my confidence, freedom and how I view the world. It also stripped me of opportunities that presented themselves. But the only thing it could not take away was my love for writing. The power to create anything with just a stroke of a pen. I wrote from ever variation of the spectrum and styles to match its effect.

    The first poem *The Disguise* started a domino effect. It was a poem so beautiful and yet so dark. That poem was the spark for future verses with a lullaby-like and musical flair. It paved a way for other epics to follow.

    Most of the poems were written a very long time ago, with the exceptions: *Social Distance, The Pandemic, Another Hundred* and *A Prayer for My Father*. This book is a time capsule back in an era when anxiety run rampant. And when *uncertainty* was all around.

CONTENTS

INTRODUCTION 1
OUT OF PLACE 4
MY OWN PRISON 7
EVER WONDER 8
THE OBSESSION 10
THE SECRET 11
WORRY ME 12
ALONE 14
NAIVETE GARDEN 16
LOST 19
A FRIEND 20
THE DISGUISE 22
ONE MORE DEATH 24
FACES 27
ANXIETY RACE 28
FALLING DOWN 30
THE BED WITHOUT DREAMS 31
NOBODY WANTS TO BE FRIENDS ANYMORE 32
WELCOME TO AMITYVILLE 35
THE PANDEMIC 36
ONLY ANXIETY 38
A MARINE OF GALAXIES 41
FOREVER MORE 42
THE MUSICAL POEM 44

SHARON	46
CONFUSION IN A CROWD	49
DEAD END	50
BROKEN HOME	54
THE SCARIES	56
PUBLIC SPEAKING	57
JUMPING SHEEP'S	58
GALLERY OF POEMS	60
EMOTION IS HACKED	62
FEAR OF THE UNKNOWN	64
BEAUTIFUL	65
SOCIAL DISTANCE	66
CLOSER EVERDAY TO DEATH	68
THE RABBIT HOLE	71
FEAR	74
FIGHT OR FLIGHT	77
TRIVIAL PERPLEX	78
ANNIE	80
SADNESS	82
AN ILLUSION	84
ADAM AND EVE'S JOURNEY	86
THE DISBELIEVER	88
REST IN POE	90
THE NOBLE POET	91
THE REJECTION EFFECTS	92
SURREAL	93

The Uncertainty from Anxiety

MY PHOBIA	94
YOU	95
OLD MAN	96
EUPHORIA	98
CENTER OF ATTENTION	100
FR3NZY PAN!C	102
THE PRISONERS	105
EVERYTHING	106
IT	107
THE COURAGE	107
CHOOSE	108
WHEN I WAS ALONE	110
NORMA'S WINDOW	112
OVERWHELMED	114
IN MY HEAD	116
ME	119
ANXIETY	120
ANOTHER HUNDRED	122
SELECTED POEMS	123
THE INSTRUMENTAL VALLEY	124
ANGRY YOUNG MEN (*VERSION 2*)	126
COVERED IN CEMENT	128
TO MY MOTHER	130
A PRAYER FOR MY FATHER	132

Jeffery Parasram

Ah fear! Ah frantic fear!
I see, I see thee near.

Ode to Fear, 1746
William Collins

The Uncertainty from Anxiety

INTRODUCTION

Move away from the crowded place
    Before the vessels burst inside!
Cast away from the human race
    Somewhere along the seaside
Avoidance of people and places
    Beyond my normalcy of thought
Transcend into a dislike within
    When everything is at a loss

Fade away from the mistic meadows
    When anxiety race to the heart
Claustrophobic in a room of shadows
    Bring me closer to the dark
Avoidance of people and places
    As things change into doubts
Constrict into these small spaces
    And learn to live without...

Jeffery Parasram

Break away just to run and hide
    From a world that cannot understands
Dangers plague from side to side
    As paranoia seems to expand
Avoidance of things and people
    Carried on for many long years
As my enthusiasm appears to trickle
    Down to the darkness with fears

Walk away from a scary time
    And disappear into the twilight
Trapped inside a life that's confine
    With invisible walls and fade sunlight
Avoidance of people and objects
    Leave me astray many times before
Seclusion taints a state of logic
    And banish souls in *forevermore*

The Uncertainty from Anxiety

Slipped away from a sudden attack
    From a fait spell in vertigo
Comatose and steer off track
    And float beside the rainbow
Avoidance of people and situation
    Form obscurity upon a dark eclipse
Cover in a cloud formation
    And sink into a quiet abyss

Dream away in the daylight hours
    As the whole world passes by
Sadness spread and then devours
    The tears of a knowing eye
Avoidance of people and setting
    Create a feeling of distrust
Ostracize with all suppressing
    And stand aside where fear abrupt

Jeffery Parasram

OUT OF PLACE

So far in between
    Further from my grasp
Parted by the remote seas
    Standing alone alas
Maroon on a land
    Stranger from a view
Reach out for a hand
    But no one wanted to

Everyone seems to connect
    With common harmony
Everybody seems to blend
    With familiar symphony
Conversation carried on
    In a social atmosphere
Talking about number one
    "Someone I couldn't be."

The Uncertainty from Anxiety

Listen from a distance
    In a curious state of mind
Imagine for an instant
    They were friends of mine
Fitting in seem impossible
    When every shoulder is cold
And something is impossible
    For a heart *without* a soul

Glance at the unfriendly faces
    With a pocket full of doubt
Wondering through the mazes
    As my assurance head south
Isolation plagues my reason
    In a climate of lost faith
Waking up from a lonely season
    Diminishes a blissful state

Jeffery Parasram

Words vocalize into echoes
      As laughter travel freely
Whisper heard from the shadows
      In a place of *uncertainty*
Out of touch in a distant place
      Where emotion fade to blue
Out of mind without a trace
      From the faces that pass you!

      And no one wanted to!
      And no one wanted to!

MY OWN PRISON

How must I release these chains?
When I can't even bear the pain

How can I break the loop?
That started in my youth

How may I leave these bars?
That carries so many scars

How can I crumble these walls?
When no one can hear my calls!

How could I finally be free?
And how will *freedom* be for me?

EVER WONDER

Ever wonder about the stars
> And the moon that follows

Ever try to locate Mars
> In the empty lunar cosmos

Ever walk in my shoes
> And look through my eyes

Feel the phobic fuse!
> As neurons burst and *collide*!

Ever hear the ripple sound
> Beam across a familiar air

It uncovers a shaky ground
> From a panic-struck scare!

Ever search for an opening
> Just to find some freedom

In the tremors that swarms in
> It awakens a knowing demon

The Uncertainty from Anxiety

Ever search for the meaning
    Of what life really means
From the stillness of morning
    To the unanswered screams!
Ever gaze for the horizon
    In hopes to find peace
From the mountains to Orion
    And the oceans with seas

Ever dream about the autumn
    And the seasons of change
In the fears which blossom
    Into a field of estrange
Ever live in the clouds
    While the world passes by
Separate from the crowd
    And the existence that died!

Ever stand in a storm

    As the eye gets closer

In the darkness that swarms

    It grows the skin colder

Ever fall in the center

    And sink into the ground

In the peak of the weather

    And the confidence that drowns

THE OBSESSION

Drowning so deep

    In my realm of dreams

It was easy to usher

    My conscience at ease

THE SECRET

The people must hear

What I must say

The world must know

What I have known

The words must show

What is true

The affectionate must feel

What is to be

The senses must savor

What awaits in Heaven

The secret must die

When the fearful lie

WORRY ME

Worry me not,
> for I have worried too long

Worry me *still*,
> for I have become ill

Worry me tears,
> for days it was hidden in screams

Worry me concern,
> for peace I could not earn

Worry me grieve,
> for all has blown in a breeze

Worry me tremors,
> for I have flee in terror

Worry me habit,
> for now, it is automatic

Worry me today,
> for it has come to stay

Worry me alone,
> for walls it has echo in stones

Worry me mistakes,
> for I have lower the stakes

Worry me years,
> for today I have accepted the same

The Uncertainty from Anxiety

Worry me temper,
    for much I could *not* mention!
Worry me senseless,
    for madness it breeds on stress
Worry me love,
    for attention I dreamt of...
Worry me money,
    for task I played the dummy
Worry me time,
    for minutes that ages in mind
Worry me death,
    for gasping a closing breath
Worry me darkness,
    for boldness that was absent
Worry me regrets,
    for the past I could not forget
Worry me change,
    for *not* staying the same
Worry me curiosity,
    for so much I could not see
Worry me dreams,
    for ambition it remains a dream
Worry me dreams,
    for ambition it remains a dream!

ALONE

To the ones I have known
    Who always I miss...
To a flower without a thorn
    That disappear in the mist

To an empty room of echoes
    That left me in the dark
To the loneliness that grows
    That bear a void in my heart

To be the one and only
    Who stand out in a crowd
To the times I felt lonely
    That kept me in the cloud

To the people I dreamt of
    In a memory fill with smiles
To a lifetime without love
    That put my feelings in exile

To the voices in my head
    That tell me, "I am alone"
From a vision of me dead
    Without a love one and home

The Uncertainty from Anxiety

To the solitude of my years
    That left me with doubts
From the lost childhood days
    That pushed everyone out

To an existence without you
    That is difficult to imagine
From the trust in your view
    That open a world for everything

To the emotional goodbye
    That takes my voice away
To the tears in my eyes
    That foresee a lonely day

To the Valentines' moments
    That show the feeling outside
To an *unlove* of chain events
    That shell the emotions inside

To the lost cold connection
    That cannot fade with time
To the feeling of isolation
    That cripple a loving mind

NAIVETE GARDEN

In a garden where
    some may know
Wonderers set sail
    from around the shore
They search for an answer
    for the loving hope
An idler from the distance
    has made his home

It was a time of flowers
    and Rainbow Roses
A sentiment of curiosity,
    I cherished alone
The cards with affectionate
    verses were in closed
It captured a moment
    of a smile so wonderful!

The Uncertainty from Anxiety

At a hesitant age
    my heart could not approach
The senses shudder
    as the eerie wind blows
In the tremors,
    I could not withhold-
I espy in a luminous array
    in the garden below

There was the amour of lovers.
    Abundant adore.
They stand on white petals
    on the sovereign throne
Is it a custom of matrimony
    or an anniversary of gold?
As the couple departed
    our spirits bear a memento
In *Naivete Garden* where boldness
    and concern may open
Many children hold hands
    in the circle of a honeycomb

Jeffery Parasram

The laughter of youthfulness
    is a smile for the old
A remembrance of yesterday
    and stories to be told

My enchantment from dawn
    has made me crave for more
In a garden by the sea
    that keep my fancy afloat
Is it a gift of affection
    only a heart can show?
Or a memory of love
    carved on a stone?
Many may venture out
    and find their own,
But for the dishearten
    They may treasure dreams alone.

The Uncertainty from Anxiety

LOST

Waiting for directions to proceed
Moving as a confuse centipede
Going down the chain of commands
Where is the Shepard to lend a hand?

Out of focus or so I may...
Lost in translation from an earlier day
Given up, what life cannot offer
Meet me by the river close to the water

Lost my sense and purpose to dream
Catching current on a vicious downstream
Rough patches are coming *ahead!*
Sense of direction goes spinning in my head

Not a map or compass to navigate
But stars that luminate from the Perlie Gates
Not a sunshine in the later noon
But an early beam from the silver moon

Jeffery Parasram

A FRIEND

A friend so far
        A friend so close
A moon with stars
        That sometime glows'

A friend who laughs
        A friend who plays
Your other half
        Is here to stay

A friend with dreams
        A friend who inspires
The golden sunbeam
        That always transpire

A friend of reason
        A friend to chance
The changing season
        Starts a romance

A friend who listens
        A friend who cares
Spirit will glisten
        And be amazed

The Uncertainty from Anxiety

A friend by choice
    A friend with faith
A time to rejoice
    And celebrate

A friend seems lost
    A friend so broken
From the *holocaust*
    Of things unspoken

A friend in need
    A friend who wants
The bitter seed
    That sometimes daunt

A friend in disguise
    A friend who pretends
The naked *lies*
    From a former friend

A friend in memory
    A friend that's gone
From the harmony
    That made them one

THE DISGUISE

Shadows of taught
    render my mind
Reminiscing
    on an imperfect time
Aversion limit
    my aspirations inside
The world I hide
    is my disguise

As the day
    becomes night
Clouds came
    closer to unite
And the ocean in the sky
    open out and cry
When rationality
    is hard to find,
And obscurity
    starts to reside
It is an insight
    I can't deny!

The Uncertainty from Anxiety

It is concealed inside,
        but it shows outside
The storms that trigger demise
        may stare you blind
In a domain where
        we strive to survive
Nothing is absolute
        when you are in denial
Certainty is wise,
        faith open eyes
The haze will drift on by
        and one day die
Causing the downpour
        to subside,
And your blissful light
        to shine

Jeffery Parasram

ONE MORE DEATH

We once lived for *infinity*
Before you drift away from me
But now a fade kiss
A fall from bliss
A wilted rose on the table
A heart not so stable
A silver tear for a moment
My love without any commitment

A pair, a couple
Emotions trapped in a bubble
Not but a gift
A love that somehow drift
One more death
Bring one last *breath*!

This will be the last of me
Deprive of this world and its beauty!
A pair, a couple
A friendly scuffle

For as the days draw near
Flash from the yesteryear

The Uncertainty from Anxiety

Say goodnight to forever deprive
Who lost their *love* for life!
Tears fall from a dark cloud
Rolling thunder out loud!
One more death
Bring one last breath...

Sleep in golden nothingness
Darkness, emptiness and blackness

You once cared about me
    Until the end of time
Partners in a tormented crime
Soon it will be
An ocean buried in a sea
Our time has come
Waiting for a heart
    With a beating drum

A pair, a couple
A heart that's muffle-

Wave a final goodbye
Pieces of petals have died
A wilted stem on the table
A feeling unstable

Jeffery Parasram

A blood red moon
A relationship doomed!
And darkness descends
Where love ends

This will be the last
    You speak to me
Emotions *still* resonate in me
Not but a tear
But a dagger shape like a spear
A flash, a minute
A soul that cannot commit
There is only animosity
A tell-tale sign of insecurity
There is only confusion
In a broken heart of illusion

Blood stained, bleak
Too difficult to speak!
A broken teared heart
Lost from the start!

FACES

Faces glance, faces judge
Without any word or a budge
Faces gaze, faces stare
All eyes are closer than appear

Faces look, faces scrutinize
Feeling of emptiness spawn inside
Faces peek, faces lie
Hidden agenda beneath their eyes

Faces spot, faces cold
Heartless emotion for the bold
Faces see, faces probe
Curious mind under the scope

Faces tell, faces frown
Uncertain ideas will inevitably drown
Faces watch, faces scare
Intimidation in the frigid air

Faces sad, faces show
Loneliness begins to grow
Faces browse, faces speculate
About the things they love and hate!

ANXIETY RACE

Shaking-falling
    And out of breath
Slowing-stalling
    Closer to death

Slipping-sinking
    And out of reach
Moving-striking
    Rapid heartbeat!

Dreading-alarming
    And out of touch
Weeping-panicking
    Worried too much

Shaking-drowning
    Out of my mind
Forgetting-cramming
    And feeling confined!

Frightening-missing
    Out of sync
Losing-stirring
    Difficult to think!

The Uncertainty from Anxiety

Crumbling-breaking
    And out of place
Daunting-feeling
    Anxiety race!

Fighting-drifting
    And out of luck
Sinking-fading
    Panic stuck!

Shaking-spinning
    Out of control
Ringing-blasting
    Thunder roll!

Running-hiding
    Out of fear
Finding-losing
    What is *real!*

Moving-slipping
    Out of hope
Racing-descending!
    On a narrow slope

Jeffery Parasram

FALLING DOWN

Distorted imagery

Out of focus

With floating objects

Uneven dimension

Ongoing flashes as colors fade

Scatter debris

With bend shapes

Skeptic place brew a false trust

Dark shadows

In a spinning world

Frail body and a lifeless feeling

Confuse faces

All mixed-up, with a clutter mind!

Paranoia spread

Envision death

Heartbeat loud and thinning air

Falling to pieces!

Unresponsive shakes

Can't stop it! Forces too strong!

Cold forehead

Numb effect

Paralyze soul!

And everything's gone!

The Uncertainty from Anxiety

THE BED WITHOUT DREAMS

In my bed, I could not sleep
I lie awake with unclosed lids
Darkness reclaimed another night
I could not vision brightness in mind
The ivory walls revealed the demon
Its shadowy movement controls my feelings

In my bed, I could not dream
The silent breeze covers my screams
This blind curse placed on the land!
It influences evil to show its hands
This misconception from within
It awakens the stream that storms within

In my bed I could not cry
The darkness spars my soul inside
The demon grows in the form of fear
My eyes are what beholds it here!

Inaccurate perception is what it feeds
Phobias reveals their silent deeds
I still lie awake with unclosed lids,
But the morning rays as always
Burn the trace of darkness

Jeffery Parasram

NOBODY WANTS TO BE FRIENDS ANYMORE

They scream and yell!

And bicker all night

With the Devil as witness

To this demeaning cry

The moon is late,

As clouds cover the ray

And their adrenaline is active,

As the rage becomes real

When you mix black and white,

It supposed to be grey,

But the result is red!

The faces of death,

As we turn away from believing

Our garden is *not* an Eden

The streets are filled with poverty

Crime escalates in the inner city-

When we turn away from our own

Nobody wants to be friends anymore!

The Uncertainty from Anxiety

It is easy for children to fall in between
When the cracks are wider than it seems
In a place where we can't agree
So, which is yours? Who is right?
As the indecision remains unknown⁻
Why do we turn away from our own?

Equality is unbalance in our mainstream
Political views are sometimes misleading
Government is *prohibited* from intervening
Music is chaotic and so is virtual games
While we point fingers on who's to blame⁻
The Republic is in question of its strength
The felonious has cast their dent
It is unsafe to step out on any day
And immorality clogs our media today
They are victims everywhere we turn
In a nation that cannot seem to learn!
As tension becomes overwhelming

Jeffery Parasram

This frustration has spark violence

Our society is on detonation

And freedom is in suppression-

Civil rights are on trial on the Promised Land

And fear controls the witness stand

As humanity separates from their own

And wonders blindly in search alone

Why must we turn away from our own?

Nobody wants to be friends anymore!

Nobody wants to be friends...

WELCOME TO AMITYVILLE

There is a house in Amityville
   That overlooks the lake and hill
Its outlook is colonial style built
   In the New York suburbs of Amityville
This house has many stories that may chill,
   And secrets that were buried within

From the remote house in Amityville
   Its residents may sometime get ill
Of ghostly remains that drains the living
   From the house that mourns in Amityville
There were eyes that peek in the windowsill,
   As the nighttime reflection reveals its sins

From the house with specters in Amityville
   Myth has it some people lost their will,
As behavior changed in the weeks that came
   From the house in turmoil in Amityville
When everything was not very still
   There was knocking and doors
     that slammed in!

From the household events in Amityville
   Residents grew weary of paranormal thrills,
And departed their home on a fearful morning
   While their belongings remain in Amityville

From the house with specters in Amityville
   From the house that bleeds in Amityville

THE PANDEMIC

Flu like symptoms
    Spreading this way
Affect many victims
    Dishearten to say!
Country on lockdown
    Panic about food
Hysteria in town
    The media conclude

Virus spread quickly
    Nowhere to hide
Save guard your family
    Keep them inside!
Dow Jones Industrial
    Massive job loss
Prove detrimental
    Culture seems lost

Global mass pandemic
    All time high
Create mass panic!
    Thousands have died!
World economic collapse
    Shortage of everything
Fear about forecast
    Keep everyone in!

The Uncertainty from Anxiety

People are falling
    Increase each day
Promote social distancing
    Keep far away!
Hospitals are crowded
    And the morgue too
World is surrounded
    By the Pandemic Flu

Way of life
    Changed forever
Pandemic strife
    Under the weather
Mask on face
    Glove on hands
A frightening place!
    A deadly *strand!*

Jeffery Parasram

ONLY ANXIETY

The doctor told me I'm healthy
But I don't believe his remedy
He said" It's only anxiety...
And anxiety never kills anybody"

But I'm not anybody, *doctor*
I am a human being not someone
In a control group
I'm an individual who wish to prosper
And not get caught up in a loop
I am trying to live a normal life
Walking with my head held high
Looking out for number one
Fixing things before it come undone

It may be easy to dismiss my words
My situation may even sound absurd at first
But I will make my stand
And maybe you will understand-
No one will ever know the things
that hurt you inside
And no one will ever see the dreams
you cast aside!

The Uncertainty from Anxiety

The things I try to fix,
When it breaks
And the nightmare I face,
When awake

So, I share with a friend my obstacle in life
And the things that breaks me, crumble inside
And she said to me "It's only anxiety,
Anxiety never kills anybody..."
But I am not anybody, *friend!*
I am a human being not someone
in a control group
I am a person who wants to put this to an end
And not get caught up in a loop

I am trying to live a normal life
Walking with my head held high
Looking out for number one
Fixing things before it come undone

No one will ever know
The things that hurt you inside!
And no one will ever see the dreams
you cast aside!
The things I try to fix,
When it breaks
And the nightmare I face,
When awake

Jeffery Parasram

I am somebody, *friends and brothers*
I am a human being, not someone
in a control group
I am an individual who wish to prosper
And not get caught up in a loop!

But no one will ever know the things
that hurt you inside
No one will ever see the dreams
you cast aside!

With the things I try to fix,
When it breaks
And the nightmare I face
When awake!

I am trying to live a normal life
Walking with my head held high
Looking out for number one
Fixing things before it come undone!

A MARINE OF GALAXIES

While the moon follows our sun
To steal its gold just for fun
The constellation clutter one by one
In the milky way where it all begun

From a place too close to our Solar System
Or maybe too far away to comprehend
The planets waltz all around
In a circular motion without an end
As the Big Bang expand our horizon

The satellites float around a planetary zone
It shows the crate on some planets
Oh, look at the damage that was done
That inflict on some orbital carelessness'

As the comet orbit our cosmos
From the vastness and to the emptiness
The universe is its frontier roads
That navigates into the openness

FOREVER MORE

Eternal thoughts ravish my mind
Follow through the end of time
Nightmare dismay and haunted soul
Spinning! Spinning! Out of control!

Childhood demon surface with age
Appear in memory tormented forever
Lifetime of regrets and closed door
Weeping! Weeping! Forever more

Unchanged season remains grey
Voices surrounds a shaded world
Ghostly phantom by the deep shore
Walking! Wondering! Into the *unknown*

Village of darkness reveal its secrets
Moonlight creatures roam the meadow
In search of life and mortal soul
Creeping! Creeping! Forever more!

The Uncertainty from Anxiety

Echoes utter from the distance
Familiar words spoken in anger
Tension abrupt many times before
Bickering! Bickering! As things unfold

Buried hopes stifles the air
Freedom resonates where spirits dwell
In an underworld the dead roam
Waiting! Waiting! Forever more

Silent necropolis covered in darkness
Fear restrained the hereafter
Death is imminent as life is a reservoir
Streaming! Flowing! By the lakeshore

Demonic forces condemned the damned
In vaulted tombs prone by eternal sins
Fate is sealed on the cold bed floor
Falling! Falling! Forever more!

Jeffery Parasram

THE MUSICAL POEM

Romantically
and always living happily!
Forever entwine in harmony
True love is a treasure
for inner beauty
That keeps us connected
Emotionally!
Ocean and river
may cross into seas
As a couple will join
into one heartbeat

Instrumentally
and composed musically!
Hear the subliminal
of its frequency!
Lost in the sound
of a loving memory
Remember this tune
with its familiarity
Acoustic wave
that travels so freely
And the musical notes
that resonate in me

The Uncertainty from Anxiety

Universally
and stars that clutter
in our galaxy
Look to the Heaven,
and what do you see?
The Cosmos defies
the force of gravity
Celestial horizon
That stretches infinitely
Show a world beyond
all its mysteries
And time with space
which move so slowly

Mystically
and appearing magically!
In the form of a smoky anomaly
Out of thin air
where no mortal would see
The hidden secrets
from The *Void Century*
Illusionists who distort
their imagery
And the sleight of hand
which foster its trickery

SHARON

I know a friend
      Whose name is Sharon
She conveys a smile
      That shows she is caring
She bears a treasure
      In her heart to send
Stories of happiness
      Stories to tell
Spirits of levity came
      Bouncing in my head
As Sharon speak of days
      She cannot forget
A gateway of stories
      A soul of diamond
A token that never
      Withered with time
Sharon is a friend
      I need not pretend
A friendship of idiom
      I did not bear in

The Uncertainty from Anxiety

The cascades of ebullient
    Cleanse a way
While the ode illustrates
    A crony play
Sharon is a friend
    We did not pretend
A friend so beautiful
    A friend so forgiving
Sharon, I promise
    A promise to bond
The world seems joyous
    From morning to dawn
It was unexpected at the time
    To understand!
Why my impulses
    Was out of my hand?
And a bond broke
    As I deserted the wagon
A harmony that should
    Have never end

So, we part ways
    Further from Heaven
A friendship that
    Should not have end
And now a absent feeling
    When I hear her name-
If Sharon was
    In my presence
I would probably
    Say to myself
"Life is worthwhile
    When you have a friend"

CONFUSION IN A CROWD

Every day, sometime
Many things seem to stray in my mind
Somehow, anywhere
The thoughts just disappear

Anyone, whomever
Seems to distract from the calm weather
Somehow, any day
I am at a loss of what to say

Every time, something
Inside me, set off a strange feeling!
Someway, anyhow
I disconnect from a crowd

Whoever, somebody
Sink my point in the unsettling seas
Everybody, someone
Chatters by flashes and sound

Anytime, everything
Stirs a suspicion from within!
Nobody, anyone
May see what their words have done

Jeffery Parasram

DEAD END

I would take a propranolol
        So, I don't have to drink alcohol
It's all about medication
        And keeping in control
The antidepressant
        Is a silent confession
As yesterday pass
        With little recollection
The caffeine is weak
        I couldn't believe
And last night
        There was so much grieve!
Sometimes I think about checking in,
        But I convince myself
It's only a game

Poe would know
        What I'm trying to bring
And I still can't find
        My passion from *within*

The Uncertainty from Anxiety

As I stood still and evaluate myself
All my ambitions
  Is thrown on the shelf
My tremors always get
  The best of me
And everything socially
  I wanted to be
When I step out
  To face the open air
There is a *fear* to step in
  And leave it out there
These signs confront
  My deepest thoughts
And the emotional warning
  I hid in the dark
The cuts that taunt
  My childhood views
It scars my belief
  With an obstruct bruise
The past is regretful
  And cannot die down!
As the turbulence and anxiety
  Rages on!

Sometimes I want to check in
> but so far away from *everything*

These symptoms have vanished
> In my only presence

And return when an
> Audience is present

My existence has been
> A practice of avoidance

While seclusion cover the wall
> With aversion

Another high pressure
> From a cold front west

An abstract feeling
> Moving to my chest

There is so much
> That was never said

When everything
> Is thrown on a shelf

Today is closer
> To a starting end

When age is further
> From a new beginning

The Uncertainty from Anxiety

Survival has been
> A learning experience

As counselors and friends
> Is sometime your best defense

There isn't time to find out why
I
  JUST
    WANT
      TO
        FIND
          A
            PIECE
              OF
                MIND!

BROKEN HOME

Broken home with a broken past
    Pulsates with anger and fear
Plates would shatter like glass
    And rained down in long tears
So much was broken in here
    And wounds that couldn't heal!
Through the years it wasn't clear
    As a child my lips were sealed

Broken home with a broken cast
    Arguing long nights of the hour
Yelling! Screaming! And moving so fast!
    Turbulence that surfaced from each other
Damages was done many times before
    Shaking! Fighting! And so much sorrow!
Outburst and pain slam many doors!
    Just to wake for an unknown tomorrow

The Uncertainty from Anxiety

Broken home with a violent clash
    Triggers the spark that flares
Tribulations of things we couldn't grasp
    About a love that wasn't there
Damages were done many times before
    And wounds that sometimes bleed!
Outburst and lashes were always cold!
    As a man my lips were seal

Broken home that seems to last
    And carry on through another day
All the elements that seem to crash!
    As happiness fade away
So many things were already lost
    In a house that wasn't a home
And all the fragments of a holocaust
    Surfaced in visions when alone!

Jeffery Parasram

THE SCARIES

It's a scary time to ever live
To walk in darkness in the cold mist
Things are changing, oh so fast!
For a culture and the mass
It's scary to think about the outcome
When? And where? It's coming from...
A scary world is a frightening place
When a child leaves without a trace

The scary thought is what comes to mind
When worrying takes up too much time
The scary truth is too hard to take
Is it better to sleep than stay awake?
Nightmare may surface when asleep
And pull you under into the deep!
A scary past may haunt for years
Break you down and feed your fears

Fear and depression are a horrible thing
The scary part is when it sinks in
The scary things may *linger* for days
It's as if you are trapped in a maze
Caught between a mountain and wall
The scary prediction is if you might fall!
The scary this and scary that
It limits your life and pull you back!

The Uncertainty from Anxiety

PUBLIC SPEAKING

Scary to even imagine

Take me away from the

Blabbing

Vocalize your problem

Panic like solemn

Confusion steps in

Voices from within

A *chill* under my skin

Apprehension flutter through

All eyes ahead

(Wishing I was dead)

Or run away instead

Public anxiety crashing

No one is clapping

Serious crowd is impatient

Wish to leave this *adjacent*

To be in another placement

Far from any event

Lost for the moment!

JUMPING SHEEP'S

I cannot seem
    to fall asleep
Pull me under
    into the deep
Wish that I
    could close my eyes
Dream away
    to the other side
So much indecision
    so long time
So much confusion
    wrapped in my mind
So many questions
    comes to light
So much restlessness,
    all through the night
Why is it difficult
    to fall asleep?
Tired of counting
    jumping sheep's

The Uncertainty from Anxiety

Wondering about
      the things that pass
Thinking why
      happiness won't last
The morning is here
      and I'm still awake
What is wrong
      with my sleep state?
The doctor prescribes
      a different sedative
Troubled it might
      become repetitive
Very few answers
      come to light
So much restlessness,
      all through the night!
Why must it be difficult
      to fall asleep?
Tired of counting
      jumping sheep's

Jeffery Parasram

GALLERY OF POEMS

I gathered all of my poems
      And stick them on the wall
Had to start my days with them
      Before I tumble and fall

The ambitions flow through me
      As adrenaline release in my veins
My pulse is a rhythm that's free
      It is without any ball and chains

An, euphoric that cannot be imagine
      Radiate in felicity for my soul
The taste I couldn't keep in
      Blow my senses out of control

Walls are covered with many verses
      With poetry that won't fade away
It is a grand scale of my universe
      For an infinite page on display

These four walls paint a history
      Handwritten poem from an earlier time
Each leaf brings a different memory
      About an *unhappy* state of mind

The Uncertainty from Anxiety

But that was then and now
    A written diary in poetic form
Chronicled the damages done
    From an era with the perfect storm

My confidence level grows stronger
    With every line that's written
But my world keeps getting *darker*
    With every new exhibition

The first poem *The Disguise*
    That ripple the domino effect
For now, it is a grand surprise
    To behold my written prospect

So, I took it upon myself
    Combining pen to paper with ink
A passion so epic to connect!
    The words of the missing link

My calling in life is clear
    As I witness my poetic gallery
Literature with a musical flair
    And all that surface in my reality

Jeffery Parasram

EMOTION IS HACKED

I don't blame anyone
    For my panic attack
But it feels much more
    As having a heart attack

Some may wonder-
    Perhaps, it's something I lack
How I get this way
    That derailed me off track

In public sometime it gets obscure
    Whenever I feel trapped
I can feel my heart racing
    With a sudden relapse!

There is bursting feeling
    With a crashing impact!
Just the thought alone
    May give a simulate cardiac!

The Uncertainty from Anxiety

It might be hard to believe
        And difficult to react
It's as if someone strike me down
        With a deadly axe

This is a mix-up reaction
        Of an unsettling abstract
This is why I seldomly
        Won't even look back!

Because eventually in my eyes
        Everything will fade to black!
In my world of unstricken danger
        Emotion is hacked

The Uncertainty from Anxiety

FEAR OF THE UNKNOWN

It is closer everyday
And grips my hand of faith
From the point of dismay
That inflict my mind state

It is the scary unknown
That brings me to my knees
From the things that's full blown
I plead for its mercy

It spread through concern
And blown into the breeze
With a panic-struck airborne
That makes me want to scream

It manipulates the senses
As it releases the fears
And drowned all confidence
Into a pitch-dark sea

It is an intense feeling
That enters into the air
With the madness that's breeding
In a panic-struck scare!

The Uncertainty from Anxiety

BEAUTIFUL

A beautiful woman becomes a bride
    A beautiful season that sometimes follows
A beautiful day with so much surprise
    A beautiful morning *without* the sorrows

A beautiful sunshine brightens the day
    A beautiful brunette smile with me
A beautiful dream from far away
    A beautiful ocean *without* a rough sea

A beautiful tune surrounds the air
    A beautiful flower blooms its petals
A beautiful love shows she cares
    A beautiful life *without* the perils

A beautiful abstract form in the clouds
    A beautiful stranger shows some kindness
A beautiful singer chorus out loud!
    A beautiful poem *without* the sadness

Jeffery Parasram

SOCIAL DISTANCE

Social distance!
Keep your distance!
From far away!
Let's say for instance
That this may be our last days
Why must it end this way?

Social distance!
Change our lives
In an instant
It's about human strives
and staying alive

Social distance!
Nobody's safe
Keep your distance
Everywhere is unsafe!
Who will be saved?

The Uncertainty from Anxiety

Social distance!
Thousands are dying!
Threatens our co-existence
Families are crying
And the number are rising

Social distance!
Wear a mask!
It's critical for your existence
How long will this last?
Pandemic is spreading fast!

Social distance!
The crowd is marching
There may be transmittance
Statues are falling
Groups are forming

Social distance!
For all my life
This was consistence
From day to night!
And these are my insight
For social distance

Jeffery Parasram

CLOSER EVERDAY TO DEATH

The luminescence fades
But why? Darkness enters
Sunbeam departed
For there is only fear
That seem to appear
May my soul rest where Angels praise
Someday it will find you...
In the end be still

May God have mercy for me
There is only the end getting closer
A burial in the garden, a tomb with a name
For all is written, on an eternal stone
Search for forgiveness, a last breath
Closer every day to death!

May my days last longer
But there is only apprehension
To *forever* drown in an eternal pit
Rest in peace
There is a final resting...

The Uncertainty from Anxiety

May the last days come slowly
Closer every day to death
There may *not* be a tomorrow
In the end death finds us
For this might be it!
Will nothingness come from the afterlife?

May my heart beat at ease
Rest in peace
As darkness consume faith
In the end be silent and still!
Worried and torn, but why?

To be forever in somber
There is only loss
A garden fill cemetery
Forever life must decay
An empty vessel without a body
The veil opens
Constant worries about death
And furthermore fading

Time is running out
The forgotten...
Closer every day to death

Lay to rest in the sculpture of Eden
Another nature tormented season
A walk in the unknown
The here and now fades
Searching for forgiveness

May my days last longer
But there is only apprehension
To *forever* drown in an eternal pit
Rest in peace
There is a final resting…

For this will be it
Closer every day to death.

The Uncertainty from Anxiety

THE RABBIT HOLE

It follows me as a reaper shadow
    Attached to me as a ball and chain
Down the rabbit hole, it will follow
    The only inhabitant that knows my name

It consumes the light of a mortal spirit
    Grab me closer and pull me down
Down the rabbit hole, knows my secret
    Take me captive in a haunted town

Away from life and everything else
    It hinders my judgement when in doubt
Down the rabbit hole, by myself!
    And find it impossible to be without...

The stage is set for what might be
    My faith it strays in a far-away place
Down the rabbit hole, bled in agony!
    So much unhappiness and few grace!

My days are chiming like as a brass bell
    The clocks are ticking and turning around
Down the rabbit hole, closer to hell!
    And all the innocence that goes down

Jeffery Parasram

THE DISLIKE YEARS

From simple days

to part years

I wonder why

it slipped away-

In dismay, I *separate*

From a world,

I could not relate

danger is real, I know!

It keeps you in

close to home.

From simple days

to frayed years.

Thoughts of darkness

shadow my reasons.

From the savage wind

To the pouring rain

And strayed in a domain

The Uncertainty from Anxiety

From simple days

to espy years

Ghosts of golden rays'

seep in. Through crevices.

There was Eden. The garden

I daydream in.

In its emerald field,

I saw a Vivid picturesque

was drawn. In the Heaven

flew the dove. From a sphere

beyond the clouds

Where freedom is autonomy

In the scope

where *Father* looks

Under. His lonely children

Wonder.

Jeffery Parasram

FEAR

It creates worries that breed anxiety
Storm from within myself
When the weather was cold and dark
Without a warning or a sign
There is a scary enemy
For when will worries and anxiety depart?

Only the irrational thoughts!
Only the dreaded perception
Fear!
Spew an intense feeling
Trigger by a sudden flash
A full-blown attack, a foot step back
Social dissociation

FEAR is drafting- *FEAR* is overwhelming!
In its mere presence
Fright!
And often revisited by worries
Create worries that breeds anxiety
Grip me in my mind
There is a fear of loss

The Uncertainty from Anxiety

An adverse effect
Precede by an aftershock
Trigger by someone or something
Fear arises!
And create worries that breed anxiety
Fall in the midst of it all
Entangled into a frightened world
Fighting! Screaming! Avoiding and fearing!

Waiting for a light of hope
To take away the trace of darkness
But there is mist, shadows and grey clouds
Hover over the horizon
Consuming the open air
Stifles the radiance of life
Killing all that is!

Fear arises!
When darkness fell
As it spread
In an open meadow
Prey on the weak
Forever in eternal fear!
Time stands still
Soulless, lifeless and helpless!

Reign in terror
Orchestrated in noise and visions
Screams in the wind
The horrific! And fearful!

May it pass soon
Lost in the wind
But why must it last forever?
It creates worries that breed anxiety
Reach for the light!
Side effects in confusion

Fear!
Returning another day
Spread its un-rational web
Fear to wandered
Afraid to try, keep a distance
For this will be it!
Fear!
Create worries that breed anxiety

The Uncertainty from Anxiety

FIGHT OR FLIGHT

Dreaded fear persists
Increased by threat
Elements of attack
Beaten down hope
Situation intense
Public awareness
Fuel the madness
Where lonely begins

Side effects notice
Pounding in myself!
Extreme emotion
When will it end?
Decision unknown
Close off normalcy
Conflicting thoughts
Provoke the mindset

Tolerate in silence
Battle in myself!
Teardrops burning
Meeting an end
Losing a fight
Just misunderstood
Faces show all
And fear remain!

Jeffery Parasram

TRIVIAL PERPLEX
(Dedicate to my fellow Guyanese going through a tough time.)

Whenever you climb
    A mountain of stress
Don't get discourage
    And get distress
Perhaps it's time
    For a long recess
Meditation may work
    Or a good night rest
And maybe you'll awake
    And feel your best!
As friends may tell you
    To have more sex
While others may comment
    To do much less-
But what *if* you feel
    An emotional oppress?
What if your world
    Was locked in a fortress?
What if your life
    Was not a true success?
How can you *fix*
    A work in progress?
Read this carefully
    Its *hot* off the press!

The Uncertainty from Anxiety

Look in the mirror
    And take a deep breath
You are beautiful
    And you are *blessed!*
Your time is coming
    With a new conquest
Live for the moment
    And don't get depress
I know how it is
    To feel helpless!
These are my thoughts
    I must confess!
And sometimes your holiday's
    Might be a mess
You are not alone
    In this *trivial perplex*
Look for the sunshine
    That sets in the West
Release your burden
    Get it off your chest
And treat yourself
    With an emotional caress
You are wonderful
    And you are *always* blessed!

ANNIE

If I could stare into her eyes
As she slowly passes by
If I could tell a story
Or read between the lines

If I could float in her seas
With the lovely gentle breeze
If I may feel so *lonely*
I would drink it from the vines!

If I may look for a friend
Who may laugh and pretend
If I could write a sonnet
And call it *Annie of Mine*

If I could foresee what happen when
In the years that made her joy end
If I could feel the glory
For winning her beautiful smile

If I may show the writing that was found
When I lost my *stable* ground
If I could hear a melody
I would hum it in my mind

The Uncertainty from Anxiety

If I could change what made her drown
From the events that circle around
If I can find a true love
And find out why it's blind

If I could find laughter in her cheeks
When I tell a humorous speech
If I may find the true meaning
Of why we keep it inside!

If I may wipe the tears off your cheeks
And bless your day with peace
If I could see the raindrops
Of a spectrum rainbow shine

If I could find a way to share
I may save you from despair
If I could float on Heavenly clouds
As they watch us passing by

If we could find a way to share
And make lonesomeness disappear
If I could bring myself to tell Annie!
Of all the dreams, I hide-my dear!

SADNESS

Fade spirit and starlight
        Swallow into blackness
Further from my sight
        Gloomy specter of repress
Follow my angst in the twilight

Falling stars from emptiness
        Orbit the horizon by satellites
Interstellar cosmos in darkness
        Form an eclipse without moonlight

Dark matter spreading in the openness
        Global transformation within the night
Consume the rays of happiness
        As it spreads in the clouds of my *sadness*

Isolated season dwell alone
        Abandon dreams of hopefulness
Windy storms with funnel cone
        Tossed in the valley of loneliness

The Uncertainty from Anxiety

Cloudy weather with dribble tone
    Fill the river of an ocean abyss
Roll of thunder strike the unknown
    And the silence and tears of my sadness

Nightmare occurs through steadiness
    Wintry elements turn to stone
Forecast certain for the loveless
    As it spread in the clouds of my sadness

Loss of faith in the arctic cold
    Consume the radiant of happiness
As it rests in the clouds of my sadness
    And the silent and tears of my sadness!

Jeffery Parasram

AN ILLUSION

As I stare upon the glowing moon
And see the clouds as it passes on through
The air is windy and sometimes cool
But mislead my senses in early youth

It is relative to what may be untrue
In the things we touch and view
What I may say or even feel
Of places and things that is *not* real-

From the pyramids of a triangular marvel
To its mythical monumental appearance
It is an elaborate setting so perfect!
In a world bind by fascination and secrets

The Uncertainty from Anxiety

There is a feeling that I can't explain
When I look beyond the thunder and rain
It perceives my thoughts with misleading things
And the images we sight is burn within

It is pertinent to express this view
From the world we *believed* that is true
What I may say or ever feel
Of places and things that is *not* real-

As I stand before a world of suspicion
The science to prove these mortal theories
It still left so many unanswered questions
From a universe which expand its mysteries

Jeffery Parasram

ADAM AND EVE'S JOURNEY

Social spirt glow with smile
    Playful emotion radiates in Heaven
Friendship stands the test of time
    Rainbow Arc in the clouds of Heaven

Dreamy spells in a rhythm state
    Lover's harmony hug and kiss
Beauty attracts a soulful mate
    Emotions connects a heart in bliss

Romance blooms a season of flowers
    Nature treasures adore by Eve
Social bees humming with wonder
    Musical garden symphony of peace

Scented candles spread an aroma
    Lavender sweetness aroused the senses
Secret passion builds an enigma
    Tempted feeling burn with incense

Goddess of Light brighten the stars
    Moonlight fairies sparkle in us
Wishes and desires blush from Mars
    Lover's circle loop around Venus

The Uncertainty from Anxiety

Couples' knot with an endless tie
    Bond together by faith and love
Devoted hearts, how could it die?
    When souls rejoin in the valley above

Prince of courage shield his woman
    From shadow that darken into fears
Hope and strength burst from Adam
    As sureness fade away her tears

Happiness grant for the lonely one
    Who kept their sprits open and true!
Prayer revise for the faithful one
    That connects a bridge made for two

Tradition restores the sacred past
    Where time and innocence stand still
Promises kept that were given to last
    From the divine hands that God fulfill

Ornamental petals filled the ceremony
    With an ambience of a picturesque wedding
Marital vows that form into prosperity
    And the praises of a new beginning...

Jeffery Parasram

THE DISBELIEVER

I want to believe
But it rolls in my sleeve
Away in oceans
Underneath the sea

So obscure and lonely
I couldn't imagine
The verse of creativity
That God put in me

Fallen from a cloud of faith
Spectrum from the Devine arc
Ascent on the surface
Illuminate my spirts for *art*

But a world uncertain
Has shadowed me
Waves so vicious!
In the violent sea

The Uncertainty from Anxiety

I slipped and tumble
From all that was lost
And gain an insight
From the meadow above

A presence of specters
Has clog my reasons
As the unbound face
Reveals a wavering season

In my loss of words
That could not surface
A syndrome so quiet
It sequels my youth
As I exist but not live
Without a knowing face

REST IN POE

Wake up! Wake up!
Poe is alive!
We are the one
Whom somehow died
Elizabeth and Annie
Had also survive
And are waiting for us
To open our eyes
Our reality exists
On the alternate side
The things we see or seem
Is it a lie? As dreams and vision
Merge in our mind
This deepened sleep shuts us blind
As we search for a reason
In a seeming time
The evidence is deceptive
To what you may find-
So, wake up! Wake up!
Poe is alive!
We are the one
Whom somehow died!
Elizabeth and Annie
Had also survive!
And are waiting for us
To open our eyes!

The Uncertainty from Anxiety

THE NOBLE POET

Maybe you could help?
I have a writer's block
I can't seem to find myself
The words are simple
But does *not* appear as yet
So, I wonder for a while
And sometimes may forget
About what I am writing
As it blanks in my head
So, I stare around the room
And scribble with my pen
As I search for the meaning
Of life and what it meant...
The minutes pass into hours
As mid-day begins to end
And the ideas are *still* sailing
Too far away to fetch
So, the hours age in days
With a small bridge of success!
And so, this is my literature!
For the dedicated noble poet
As many may question my reasons
Of an author's passion and regret
And the novels that must be written
From novelist who dream about it

Jeffery Parasram

THE REJECTION EFFECTS

Refuse the offer to what may be said
    Dismiss my emotions, as it doesn't matter
Turn it down and walk away
    Negative effects for the latter

I went away and felt abandon
    My mind was strong, or so it seems
Fall into a pit without a bottom
    And all was lost inside of me!

I ponder the days wake in the night
    Felt unworthy just to be around!
The tunnel is dark without any light
    And friends were asking what was wrong

The days were long and so alone
    Rejected from love and all its affection
Thrown in a gutter and cover with stones
    And these are my *written* confessions!

Watching the screen in my head
    It recaps that day over and over!
Listening to the words that was said…
    It turned your spirit colder and colder!

SURREAL

It keeps me up at night
Breaking me, shaking me
Trembling in me
In a spiral down
The icy nerve
Freezes my finger
As madness hit my heart
Rushing my veins
Under my skin, it lives *again*!
Reacting with every move
Appear into the open
As a sudden feeling
It grabs me with fright!
Controlling me-fighting the beast!
Lost in myself
Pores are cold
Bending my soul
And overwhelm my mind
Visible through my senses
It is real!
Want to flee
God, want to flee!
Everything is surreal...

Jeffery Parasram

MY PHOBIA

I am the pieces of my phobia
    Scattered through the course of time
Blown apart by the supernova
    And the emptiness that comes to mind

I am the influence of my phobia
    Who sedate the forces from within
I try to reach the field of utopia
    But fall into the depth of my sins

I am the meaning of my phobia
    That set me apart from the everyday
Situation filled my paranoia
    Of an event that won't go away!

I am the effect of my phobia
    Persist in the earliness of my age
From all the days of a childhood trauma
    Result in the projected stage

I am the dreams of my phobia
    Oblivious from the nexus of life
Asleep in the realm of my coma
    Unattended to the world outside

I am the scent of my phobia
    That emits into the frigid air
It is a reminder of a familiar aroma
    And the fear that clouds me everywhere

The Uncertainty from Anxiety

YOU

Shut off from the open
Many words unspoken
To another human
The only thing certain
Is you, without you?
I am on my own
In a place that's broken
Between a man and woman
A heart of misfortune
That drown my emotions
A I stand alone
And think about you

Lost in her maze
Afar from touching
From nigh time through the day
Everyone seems unwilling
As my reasons turn to grey
A taught about dreaming
And the romance about change
My days seem lifeless
As I exist without living
The moral of my being
Is absorb in L____Ann Kim
And every day is ending
As I wait for a friend

OLD MAN

Old man-old man!
    What have you done?
Sleeping in a coma
    From the evening sun

Old man-old man!
    What did you do?
Fighting the urges
    That's inside of you

Old man-old man!
    Why do you cry?
Talking about dying!
    In your early life!

Old man-old man!
    Living a lie
Always in denial
    To the knowing eye

Old man-old man!
    You know it's true
Living in solitude
    In a shadow room

The Uncertainty from Anxiety

Old man-old man!
>Look at your window

The world is moving fast!
>As you are moving slow

Old man-old man!
>Talk in your sleep

Ghostly character
>Spawn in your dreams

Old man-old man!
>Leave me alone

I don't have another
>In this broken home

Old man-old man!
>Why do you curse?

Anger is controlling
>I can see you burst!

Jeffery Parasram

EUPHORIA

The fears have passed and taken its affect
As darkness fade away from the morning sunset

Demons have perished for their eternal sins
As the Sunday morning service begins

Guns and tanks have become obsolete
While the forces of nature retreat

Inequality collapse in the hazy fields
While people join together as human beings

Presidents are impeached in their country
As one voice speaks to the many

Diseases are eradicated in the hands of faith
As miracles evolve from the prayer that save...

The Uncertainty from Anxiety

Sadness translates into happiness
Because God's love is endless!

Nightmare have disappeared from our thought
As dreams filled the void with joy

Material builds on the wants of our needs
But affection is the only treasure we need

Solitary confines the helpless and the loneliness
But freedom releases every emotion in bliss

Hope lifts the spirit of a fallen victim
As many things are possible in Eden

Jeffery Parasram

CENTER OF ATTENTION

To be the one
In the center of it all
I never knew
Or how to react
As I felt *trapped*
By the enclosure
From the cubic wall

To be the one
That feels out of place
And cannot connect
To a common audience
It disconnects love
Even in childhood
As I have not learned
How to fit in

To be the one
That is the focus of
Who stands so close
But feels so far
From the beings
That gather around
In the presence
Of a confounding thought!

The Uncertainty from Anxiety

To be the one
In the middle of a crowd
Who cannot blend
Or shadow a doubt
It is a dislike state
Of overwhelming reasons
That covers a spirit
Inside an obscure cloud

To be the one
In the circle of a spotlight
That give off negative
As uncertainty follows within
Helplessness is abounding
As mercy fill the soul-
God let there be hope
For the ones trapped inside!

Jeffery Parasram

FR3NZY PAN!C

Can you feel my heart how it beats?
Can you see my soul how it seeps?
Can you hear my sounds as it breach?

Well, I know what you think
As my eyelid make me blink
And I feel all the needles
How it perspires this fever

I can hear what they say about me
And I know it's *not* easy to be free!
Have you ever really tried?
And just run away and hide,
Or did it make you want to cry?

Its moving fast, as the freight train pass
Its moving fast with every hour pass
Its moving fast with the thumping of my heart
Moving fast-fast-fast, as the frigid draft pass!

Well, I have all the symptoms
And feel as a victim
In a place I can't mention
Why I feel so *different*!

The Uncertainty from Anxiety

Its moving fast,
    as the freight train pass
Moving fast-fast-fast!
    with every minute pass!
Moving fast-fast-fast!
    with the thumping of my heart!
Moving fast-fast-fast!
    as the frigid draft pass!

With this madness-make me frantic
In a time, I cannot keep it
I cannot even hide it
With this pulse of frenzy panic!

Well, I have all the reason
And I can't confront the demon
When I am in a place of confusion
All I think about is *leaving*!

It's moving fast,
    as the freight train pass
Moving fast-fast-fast!
    with every second pass!
Moving fast-fast-fast!
    with the thumping of my heart!
Moving fast-fast-fast!
    as the frigid draft pass!

With this madness made me frantic
In a time, I cannot grab it!
I cannot even hide it!
With this pulse of frenzy panic!

Well, I have all the reason
And I can't confront the demon
When I am in a place of confusion
All I think about is *leaving*!

Moving Fast! Fast! Fast!
   As the freight train pass!
Moving fast-fast-fast!
   As the frigid draft pass!

With this madness made me frantic
In a time, I cannot grab it!
I cannot even hide it!
With this pulse of frenzy panic!

THE PRISONERS

Dogs on a leash

Parrots in a cage

Fish in an aquarium

Mice in a lab

Cows in a barn

Lions in a cage

Dolphins in a pool

Pigs in a sty

Chickens in a fence

Cats in a house

Rabbits in a hutch

Sheep's in a fold

Horses in a hedge

Puppies in a pen

Agoraphobics in their home

EVERYTHING

Apprehension lives inside of anxiety.
Creating misery and distrust wherever
it dwells. Holding certainty at bay. As it
Cloud judgement, it fills the perception
with delusive observation that appears
Rational. The seed is convincing
That it plants.

Imposing deluded thoughts that
bloom uncontrollable in a conscious mind.
The trailing vines feeds on certitude
Of a soul. Taking away the spark
within as it consumes all assurance.
Containing all that is pure, and fighting
to control everything. Suppressing
everything. Killing everything that was
good.

The Uncertainty from Anxiety

IT

Just to face today
    It leaves me sobbing
Just to find a way
    It leaves me guessing
Just to keep still
    It leaves me shaking
Just to concentrate
    It leaves me wondering
Just to sleep so late
    It leaves me tossing
Just to fall away
    It keeps me falling

THE COURAGE

Walk proud
    Hold on
Talk loud
    Be strong
Push back
    Be courageous
Fight back
    And victorious!

Jeffery Parasram

CHOOSE

Good and evil
    Black or white
Kill the devil
    Make it right

Hot and cold
    Love and hate
Make it unfold
    Let them relate

Fight or flight
    Dead or alive
Feel the fright!
    Who will survive?

Rain or sunshine
    Night and day
Seems to entwine
    Changes everyday

Friend or foe
    Peace or war
Fallen below
    Open a scar

The Uncertainty from Anxiety

Odd or even
    Always or never
Change of season
    Gone forever

Fear or courage
    Predator or prey
May discourage
    Fade to gray

Fact or fiction
    Poetry or prose
Create a friction
    Sprout a rose

Forgive or blame
    Agree or refuse
Fuel the flame
    Time to choose!

Joy or sorrow
    Gain or loss
Gone tomorrow
    All is lost!

Jeffery Parasram

WHEN I WAS ALONE

When the world refuse to shine
In a cloudy era when I was blind

A sudden burst from in the air
It cascades the Heaven on a torrent day

From a dreary season of heavy pour
It washed on to our concrete shore

From remnants of petals so far from home
My days to ponder, when I was alone

From whispers of degrees that may succeed
In a loss of words that drown in deep sea

An avoidance of events that washed away
A sinful reminder of yesterday

The Uncertainty from Anxiety

A sense of happiness that may dissever
In peace and harmony that pulls me under

From journey and trifles so far from home
My days to wonder, when I was alone

A childhood storm with rolls and thunder
In a loss of thoughts that pulls me under

An ocean that reflects within my hands
It streams across an aquatic land

My castaway in a singular path
It paved a way for an uncommon *art*

My yesteryears is what I found
A childhood literature capture in sound

Jeffery Parasram

NORMA'S WINDOW

When Norma was
    Wandering alone
There was so much
    she had never known
She could not find
    a safe place to go
So, Norman got accustomed
    to staying at home.
She never gasps by heart
    how to grow,
she was too fainthearted
    to wonder offshore.
"No!" she said,
    "My fear is spreading more,
And my days
    Are getting old!"
She got trapped
    In a housebound show
Which haunted
    Her secure soul.
It's been 14 Years
    She ignored.

The Uncertainty from Anxiety

Norma played
> The separate role.

She is the person who views
> Her world from the window.

The sunbeam would
> Shine like gold,

When inside
> Is dark and Cold,

As January cool air
> Form snow.

Tonight, ivory Heaven
> Land on the globe.

But Norma knows only half
> The mystery is shown.

Maybe tomorrow she would find a reason
> To venture out the Door.

Because only part of the picture
> Is reveal through Norma's window.

Jeffery Parasram

OVERWHELMED

Intensify by anxiety

For a single fraction

Thrown off by a mere distraction

An overwhelming affect

Surface to eye level

Awaken by a distraught devil

Feeling of being overwhelmed

Time of severe stress

Wish to lay my head to rest

But it infects all thoughts

Difficulty to focus!

A cloud of locus

Invade every fiber of my being

Experience a lack of hope

Moving down an unsteady slope

Broken up in pieces

An irrationality starts to bloom

A terrible doom!

Taken over all of my life!

Consuming more and more!

Reaching the inner core

Fear out of control

The Uncertainty from Anxiety

Compound with thoughts

The things I cannot

Defeat by an unknown face

Heighten with a keen awareness

But far from sureness

Complexity of the situation

Very strongly affects

Too many visuals intersect

At the exact time

The senses submerge

The confusion surges!

Overload the cerebral system

Often many things would stem

Bewildered by chain of events

Initiated an excessive

Psychological strain

Follow by a mental drain

Jeffery Parasram

IN MY HEAD

Every thought and emotion
Comes from a source and notion
That travel to my head
I cannot control it, or even explain it...
As it keeps me up in bed
Only to make me wonder
Where? When? And how?
It gets in my head!
My passion is calling
The sentence is forming
As I penned the verse
And arrange it in sequence
To the point of perfection
It is down to a science!

I drowned myself in the design
Obsess for the results
It moves me far ahead
As I get lost sometimes
The visions have project
As my conscience interpret-

The Uncertainty from Anxiety

But the message is unclear!
And in the dawn, I am drained
As I often think about...
When? Where? And how?
It gets in my head

2

In my head
The signs are dim
As I am often mis-lead
By the daily things
From the objects ahead

In my head
Everything is cast down
To the point of regret
As I often found
And the steps I withheld

Jeffery Parasram

In my head

Things get carried away

As I let it spread

In the mind state I stray

And the thoughts I embed

In my head

The prediction is true

As I often mis-read

From this point of view

And the reality I dread

The Uncertainty from Anxiety

ME

How does it feel to be me?
When I cannot break free
I write most days
From the dismay of life
I look around at our ruinous ways
And I weep! And I weep!
So, who are you to tell me
About it anyway?
I try to sleep!
And want to dream
As I try to figure out
How to get away
From the anxiety that shake my knees
At any given day let me speak!
Before my time is complete
And before you turn away
Let me tell you about me!
And the unwritten poetry
That surface in my dream
Before I go away
This is how I feel-
Who are you to tell me?
Still waiting to be heal
From the fragments of my fears
To the elements in me

ANXIETY

Anxiety! Anxiety!
    What may I say?
It leaves me speechless
    Just to talk today

Anxiety! Anxiety!
    Pulsate my vein
It left me shaking
    Just to keep so still

Anxiety! Anxiety!
    Confuse my day
It leaves me wondering
    Just to concentrate

Anxiety! Anxiety!
    Make me turn away
It left me guessing
    Just to find a way

The Uncertainty from Anxiety

Anxiety! Anxiety!
    Why do you play?
It left me losing
    Just to foul this game

Anxiety! Anxiety!
    Why do you stay?
It leaves me sobbing
    Just to face today

Anxiety! Anxiety!
    Controls my brain
If left me disabled
    Just to function okay

Anxiety! Anxiety!
    Keep me awake
It left me tossing
    Just to sleep

Jeffery Parasram

ANOTHER HUNDRED

I submit my poems
To the Library of Congress
I never realize, it would reach *another 100*
A hundred reasons to live for today
The cold harsh seasons
That *almost* made me fade away
It's hard to imagine, I made it this far
Through the dark horizon
There is a shooting star!
My day is today, And not tomorrow
I must give it a *100!* Before I let go
Don't ever give less than *100* percent
And always be blessed
For that special moment
The best things in life
May only come once,
So, cease the moment before it's gone!
A century of writing
Or so it feels, passes so quickly
As time will heal...
The things that were broken
And needed to be fix
Made up a *100*
On my bucket list

The Uncertainty from Anxiety

SELECTED POEMS

Jeffery Parasram

THE INSTRUMENTAL VALLEY
(Dedicated to the heroes and victims of

September 11, 2001.)

In earliness of a darken day
    As far as my eyes can see
When the hours begin to turn grey
    From the Heaven, Earth and Seas
For love ones that passed away
    And leave us in the stone alley
While the Angels guide their wings
    Into the Instrumental Valley

When the season change its brilliance
    In the morning that shook me
It was a day of unexpected occurrence
    That brought us to our knees
As the call made its connections
    In the closing words with tears
Our hearts were fill with mixed emotions
    Outside the Instrumental Valley!

The Uncertainty from Anxiety

As the forecast revealed a dust of cloud
    On the towers in the marble city
There was a crumble so loud!
    It rained death and crystal debris-
But the saints guide the crowd
    One by one through the horrific scene
And the sprits glow with *September love!*
    Inside the Instrumental Valley

And so, the valley hymn with colorful songs
    In an orchestrated rhythm for peace
It chants from United Air to the Pentagon
    With the harmony to set them free
As the keyboard tune to a universal sound
    Our Creator fine tuned the melodies
And the musical notes resonate all around
    Inside the Instrumental Valley

    The Kingdom of our Almighty!

Jeffery Parasram

ANGRY YOUNG MEN (*VERSION 2*)

Follow the fighting scream
    And anyone may find them
In a violent epidemic chaos
    Between men verses men
It is reality in today's world
    Of an increasing trend
Among the bloody wars
    Escalated by young men
It is a burning rage!
    That spread in the hundreds
The soaring crime rates
    Has elevated again-
And these are the statistics
    Of angry young men

Their blood is composed of fury
    With a burning venom
As their spirit wonder about
    In a darker realm
Their hands are grip tight
    To a deadly weapon
As their mindset is stirred
    Into getting *even*

The Uncertainty from Anxiety

They left a trail of evidence
    About their lifeless victim
On the doorway of society
    To find a way to comprehend
And these are the killing's
    Of angry young men!

The inedible is balancing
    As it weighs on the jury stand
For a young boy to be sentence
    With the chain on his hands
Prison is a duration
    Inside a barricade of chance
Another child has fallen!
    Into the system that strand...
Angry young men are the carriers
    In a violent restricted land
Their temper is a driving force
    That flicker to the bitter end-
And these are the regrets
    Of angry young men
And these are the trend
    Of angry young men!

Jeffery Parasram

COVERED IN CEMENT

The developer bought in
    their machinery
And wipe out everything
    we used to see
The forest appeared more
    as a Death Valley
From the center of town
    In the heart of Bowie!
They talk about
    A future investment
Without the worry of
    Environmental consequences
As they paved a path
    For a new street
It was treated
    With gravel and concrete-
What happen to this garden
    Of nature's ornament?
That dress the forest
    With its green acre tent-

The Uncertainty from Anxiety

And as the *Notice* show
    Signs of development
All the pastures were
    Covered in cement

The suburb transforms
    Into an urban view
With traffic and lights
    That clutter the avenues
Structures elevate from
    The foundation to the roof
As bricks filled the corner
    Of nature's scenic view
Wildlife slowly fades away
    From the modern sediment
It seems that nature's frontier
    Eventually comes to an end
And as the *Notice* show
    Signs of development
All the pastures were
    Covered in cement

Jeffery Parasram

TO MY MOTHER
(Dedicate to my wonderful mother

Evelyn Parasram.)

Greetings to you an amazing lady

Caring traits to the Virgin Mary

Blessed to have you as my mother

Who spark my childhood with joy and wonder!

A beautiful life with dreams and harmony

A sunlit forest with a festival of ceremonies

A heart that beats to a loving rhythm

A happiness that shines as a colorful prism

Thank you for the memorable years

And the times you show how much you care

You propel me to reach for the stars!

To break from a world plague by scars

My father inscribes about your peaceful soul

A heart of diamond fashioned in gold

His journal captured the essence in you

As his eyes was lost in love that's true!

The Uncertainty from Anxiety

I know about the dismals in your heart
The malignant that tore your world apart
But you achieve it through the Grace of God
And harness the energy with a lightning rod

You triumphed over the obstacles of life
The miracles in you heal all your strives
All and all your spirits were high
As all the shadows seem to pass on by

August came with a new reminder
And all the hopes of a pleasant November
Your victories will reign from the Divine hand
And you shall *prosper* where ever you stand!

Jeffery Parasram

A PRAYER FOR MY FATHER
(1947-2020)

Dear Lord, who created the Heaven and Earth
    The Shepard who gave purpose to my life
Scriptures that grant my heart self-worth
    And the undying love of Jesus Christ

I am forever grateful for the worldly gifts
    The harvest that takes root in the fertile ground
Its season that changes as the clouds adrift
    And the Arc is where God's promise is found

I ask for you beyond the nebulous of stars
    Where Angels dwell in the Kingdom of Heaven!
I pray for my father in the evening star
    To reach your faith in the refuge of Haven

The Throne of God and the Mighty Lamb
    Oh, how I worship your everlasting grace
I pray for my father Cecil Parasram!
    From the great beyond to the Pearlie Gates!

The Uncertainty from Anxiety

Cecil gospel was to live a life without greed
    Free your soul from the elements that corrupt
Plant your forest with a divine set of seeds
    And harvest your life with a better crop

My father smiles with the rest of the world
    His laughter attracts a sea of viewers
The happiness he brought was a rare pearl
    And jokes were a jewel for his sarcastic humor

His spirit was high with a love for life
    The aura he radiates was a priceless Jem
He furnished a world with his loving wife
    A marriage forever that branch many stems

Lord! Please let him hear the prayers we send!
    And the love that bear from our hearts
Please guide him to his family and friends
    When a moment in time may seem too dark!

Jeffery Parasram

The haze will drift on by
And one day die
Causing the down pour to subside
And your blissful light to shine

The Uncertainty from Anxiety

SPECIAL THANK YOU

South America, Guyana has seen the second highest suicide rate in the world. I would like to give a special thanks to the men and women helping to curb this epidemic. Your dedication and love are very much appreciated!

Jeffery Parasram

The Uncertainty from Anxiety

www.ingramcontent.com/pod-product-compliance
Lightning Source LLC
LaVergne TN
LVHW011423080426
835512LV00005B/225